LOVE AND DEVOTION SERIES

*All We
Have Lacked
is God*

THE

BAPTISM

OF LOVE

*Truths compiled
from the writings of*

FRANCIS
FRANGIPANE

ISBN #1-886296-09-X

Copyright © 1994 Francis Frangipane
Arrow Publications
P.O. Box 10102
Cedar Rapids, IA 52410

CONTENTS

1.

BEWARE OF COLD LOVE

Is your love growing and becoming softer, brighter, more daring, and more visible? Or is it becoming more discriminating, more calculating, less vulnerable, and less available? This is a very important issue, for your Christianity is only as real as your love is. A measurable decrease in your ability to love is evidence that a stronghold of cold love is developing within you.

Guard Against Unforgiveness!

"Because lawlessness is increased, most people's love will grow cold" (Matt 24:12). A major area of spiritual warfare that has come against the church is in the sphere of church relationships. Satan knows that a church divided against itself cannot stand. We may enjoy temporary blessings and seasonal breakthroughs, but to win a citywide war, Jesus is raising up a united, citywide church. An earmark of this corporate, overcoming church will be its commitment to love. Yet, because of the increasing iniquity in the end of this age, true Christian love will be severely assaulted.

There is no spiritual unity, and hence no lasting victory, without love. Love is a passion for oneness. Bitterness, on the other hand, is characterized by a noticeable lack of love. This cold love is a demonic stronghold. In our generation, cold love is becoming increasingly more common. It shuts down the power of prayer and disables the flow of healing and outreach. In fact, where there is persistent and hardened unforgiveness in a person or church, the demonic world (known in Matthew 18:34 as "torturers") has unhindered access.

The Scriptures warn that even a little root of bitterness in a person's life can spring up and defile many (see Hebrews 12:15). *Bitterness is unfulfilled revenge.* Another's thoughtlessness or cruelty may have wounded us deeply. It is inevitable that, in a world of increasing harshness and cruelty, you will at some time be hurt. But if you fail to react with love and forgiveness, if you retain in your spirit the debt the offender owes you, that offense will rob your heart of its capacity to love. Imperceptibly, you will become a member of the majority of end-time Christians whose love is "growing cold."

Bitterness is a classic symptom of the stronghold of cold love. To deal with this, you must repent of this attitude and forgive the one who hurt you. This painful experience was allowed by God to teach you how to love your enemies. If you still have unforgiveness toward someone who hurt you, you have failed this test. Fortunately, this was just a test, not a final exam. You actually need to thank God for the opportunity to grow in divine love. Thank Him that your whole life is not being swallowed up in bitterness and resentment. Millions of souls are swept off into eternal judgment every day without any hope of escaping from embitterment, but you have been given God's answer for your pain. God gives you a way out: *love!*

As you embrace God's love and begin to walk in forgiveness, you are actually pulling down the stronghold of bitterness and its manifestation of cold love in your life. Because of this experience, you will eventually have more love than you ever did. You truly do need to thank God.

Love Without Commitment Is Not Love

"And at that time many will fall away and will deliver up

one another and hate one another. And many false prophets will arise, and will mislead many. And because lawlessness is increased, most people's love will grow cold" (Matt 24:10-12).

I want to make it perfectly clear: there is no such thing as love without commitment. The measure of your love is found in the depth of your commitment. How often I have heard people tell me, "I loved once, but I was hurt." Or, "I was committed to Christian service, but they used me." People withdraw from being committed, never realizing that their love is growing cold! It may not *seem* like they have become cold—they still go to church, read the Bible, tithe, sing and look like Christians—but inside they have become distant and aloof from other people. They have withdrawn from the love of God.

Jesus said, **"It is inevitable that stumbling blocks come"** (Matt 18:7). In your walk there will be times when even good people have bad days. As long as you live on earth, there will never be a time when **"stumbling blocks"** cease to be found upon your path. *People do not stumble over boulders, but over stones— little things.* To stumble is to stop walking and fall. Have you stumbled over someone's weakness or sin lately? Have you gotten back up and continued loving as you did before, or has that fall caused you to withdraw somewhat from walking after love? To preserve the quality of love in your heart, you must forgive those who have caused you to stumble.

Every time you refuse to forgive or fail to overlook a weakness in another, your heart not only hardens toward them, it hardens toward God. You cannot form a negative opinion of someone (even though they may deserve it!) and allow that opinion to crystallize into an attitude. For, every time you do, an aspect of your heart will cool toward God. You may still think you are open to God, but the Scriptures are clear: **"the one who does not love his brother whom he has seen, cannot love God whom he has not seen"** (1 John 4:20). You may not like what someone has done, but you do not have an option to stop loving them. Love is your only option.

What do I mean by love? First, I do not merely mean "tough love." I mean gentle, affectionate, sensitive, open, persistent love. God will be tough when He needs to be, and we will be firm when He tells us to be, but beneath our firmness must be an underground river of love waiting to spring into action. By "love" I mean a compassion that is empowered by faith and prayer to see God's best come forth in the one I love. When I have love for someone, I have predetermined that I am going to stand with them, regardless of what they are going through.

We each need people who are committed to us as individuals—people who know we are not perfect, but love us anyway. The manifestation of God's kingdom will not come without people being committed to each other to reach God's fullness. We are not talking about salvation; we are talking about growing up in that salvation until we love and are committed to each other with Jesus' love.

Many people will stumble over little faults and human weaknesses. These minor things are quickly pumped up by the enemy into great big problems. Oh, how frail are the excuses people use to justify withdrawing from others! In reality, these problems, often with a church or pastor, are a smoke screen which mask the person's lack of love.

We need to overcome our hangups about commitment, for no one will attain the fullness of God's purposes on earth without being committed to imperfect people along the way.

"Well, as soon as I find a church that believes as I do, I will be committed." This is a dangerous excuse, because as soon as you decide you do not want to forgive, or God begins to deal with the quality of your love, you will blame your withdrawing on some minor doctrinal difference. The kingdom of God is not based on mere doctrines: it is founded upon *relationships*—relationships with God and, because of God, with one another. Doctrines only help define those relationships. We are not "anti-doctrine," but we are against *empty* doctrines, which seem like virtues but are simply excuses that justify cold love.

The Greatest Commandments

An expert in the Law once asked Jesus which was the greatest commandment. His reply was wonderful. He said,

"You shall love the Lord your God with all your heart, and with all your soul, and with all your mind, and with all your strength" (Mark 12:30).

Jesus then said, **"The second is this, 'You shall love your neighbor as yourself"** (v 31). When you love God, your love for others will be like your love for God: *the second is like the first.* The more you unconditionally love God, the more you will unconditionally love others.

To those whose attitude is "just Jesus and me" I say, it is wonderful you found Jesus. But you cannot truly have Jesus and simultaneously not do what He says. *The outgrowth of love and faith in Christ is love and faith like Christ's*, which means we are committed, even as He is, to His people.

You see, the kingdom of God is not in you or in me. It is in *us,* corporately. We are being perfected into a unit (see John 17). To have the kingdom, we must be committed to one another as individuals and as churches. If Christ

Notes

Very Important

11

accepts us while we are still imperfect, we must also accept one another. *The people who possess the kingdom of God in its reality are people who overcome the obstacles of each other's faults.* They help each other become what God has called them to be: the living body of Jesus Christ.

Remember, the goal of pulling down the stronghold of cold love is to see the oneness of Christ's body revealed. You will be challenged in this, but if you persist you will discover the heights and depths, the length and breadth of Christ's love. You will become a body filled and flooded with God Himself.

2.

LOVE: GOD'S PRESERVATIVE

There will be a time when each of us will stand before Jesus Christ and He will open a door called "reality-past." There, we shall gaze into the days of our earthly existence.

Jesus will not only commend our lives in a general way, but He will point to specific things we did. Rejoicing together with us, He will say of them, "Well done!" Perhaps there was a special act of kindness that turned a bitter person back toward God; or you will have overcome your fears and led a person to Christ whom God then used to win thousands.

In the Latin translation of the Bible, the phrase "well done" is rendered "Bravo!" How would you like Jesus to say that to you? Imagine Him with His arm around your shoulder saying, *"Bravo! You were just an average person, but you trusted Me, you learned to love without fear, and look how many hearts we touched together!"* To be so pleasing to Christ that He rejoices over the life we give Him should be our highest goal.

Love in the Midst of Pressure

Yet, it is here, in a world filled with devils, devil-possessed people and conflicts of all sorts, that we must find the life of Christ. In fact, when Jesus warned about the Great Tribulation, one meaning of the word "tribulation" is "pressure." Even today, is not stress and pressure increasing upon people? In spite of these tensions, God has called us to love *extravagantly*. If we do not counteract the stress of this age with love, we will crumble beneath the weight of offenses.

Have you ever seen in a supermarket a shopping cart full of bent food cans? Most have lost their labels. You can buy a half dozen for a dollar or two. What happened is that the atmospheric pressure outside the can was greater then the pressure inside, and the can collapsed. It could not withstand the pressure.

Similarly, we must have an aggressive force pushing out from inside us that is equal to the pressures trying to crumble us from the outside. We need the pressure of God's love pouring out through us, neutralizing the pressure of hatred and bitterness in the world.

Love is God's preservative. It surrounds our souls with a power greater than the power of the devil and the world around us. It keeps us balanced; it insulates us against the hostility that exists in our world. Love is the shelter of the Most High; it is the substance of the place of immunity.

Lord, forgive me for looking for some other means of protection besides love. Truly, pressures have increased upon my life; stress multiplies daily in our world. Yet, Lord, grant me the eternal equalizer: love. Grant that I would walk in such surrender to You that the power of Your love would unceasingly emanate from my soul. Amen.

Notes

3.

THE BAPTISM OF LOVE

To Dwell upon God

It is hard for us in this anxious, fearful age to quiet ourselves and meditate upon God in our hearts. We can engage ourselves with Bible study or other acts of obedience; in varying degrees we know how to witness, exhort, and bless. We know how to consider these things, and even perfect them. But to lift our souls above the material world and consciously dwell upon God Himself seems beyond the reach of our Christian experience.

Yet, to actually grasp the substance of God is to enter the place of immunity;

it is to receive into our spirits the victory Christ has won. For His sake, we cannot content ourselves merely with good works. Ultimately, we will discover that study and church attendance are but forms that have no satisfaction in and of themselves. These activities must become what the Lord has ordained them to be: *means through which we seek and find God.* Our pleasure will be found not in the mechanics of spiritual disciplines, but that these disciplines bring us closer to the Almighty.

Paul's cry was, **"that I may know Him"** (Phil 3:10). It was this desire to know Jesus that produced Paul's knowledge of salvation, church order, evangelism and end time events. Out of his heart's passion to know God came revelation, the writing of Scriptures and knowledge of the Eternal.

Paul's knowledge was based upon his *experience* with Christ. Yet, we have satisfied ourselves with a system of historic *facts* about God without pressing into the *reality* of God. The very purpose of the Bible's inspiration is to compel us to find the living God. If the Scriptures have not transferred to us this basic desire for God, our relationship to the Word of the Lord is too superficial.

Our goal is to seek earnestly for God until we find Him. Theological knowledge is merely the first step toward the place of immunity; it is the map which leads to the country. For too long we have argued concerning the doctrinally-correct way to approach God, without truly entering His Presence ourselves. We debate the proper way to interpret the map God has given us without genuinely embarking on the journey.

Love Which Surpasses Knowledge

There is a place greater than knowledge where we abide in Christ's love. This is, indeed, the place of immunity. The apostle's prayer for you and I is that we would **"know the love of Christ which surpasses knowledge"** (Eph 3:19). There is a dwelling place of love that God desires us to enter. It is a place where our knowledge of God is fulfilled with the substance of God.

We cannot truly know God without, in some way, also experiencing His Person. If you had never seen a sunrise or a starry night sky, could any description substitute for your own eyes beholding their expansive beauty? Likewise, to truly know God we must seek Him until we pass through our knowledge into an encounter with the Almighty.

The "upward call" of God draws us through our doctrines into the certainty of the Divine Presence. The journey leaves us in the place of surrender, where we yield our being into His hands. We must learn how to listen to Him and, from listening, ascend higher to the dwelling place of love.

The last great move of God in the earth shall be distinguished by overwhelming love, *a baptism of love,* poured out from Christ to His people and returned again, with our praise, back to Him. For those who truly yearn for Jesus there shall come, in ever-increasing waves, Christ's deep, fulfilling love.

Yes, His cross shall break us; indeed, His holiness shall purify us. But it shall be His love that floods our being with Himself.

Is this possible, my Lord? Is it true that I might know the love of God which surpasses all knowledge? Oh God, I seek to know You, to live in the substance of Your love. For Your love is the stronghold of my protection.

Help me, Master, to recognize Your love, not as a divine emotion, but as Your very substance! Help me to see that it was neither Pilate nor Satan that put You on the cross; it was love alone to which You succumbed. Remind me again that it is Your love which still intercedes for me even now. Amen.

You knew before me what I was like
You know you were going to the cross before you left heaven, You made it possible for us to go to heaven by your sacrifice on the cross
What Great Love!

19

4.

FORGIVENESS AND THE FUTURE OF YOUR CITY

The redemptive power of God is released when people forgive each other. Individuals, families, churches, and even the atmosphere of a city can change when pardon is released. When such a display of grace is poured out, principalities and powers are neutralized, often without so much as speaking a word against them.

The Power in Forgiveness

Perhaps nothing so typifies the transforming, cleansing power of God as that which is experienced when a soul receives forgiveness. It is the power of new life, new hopes, and new joy. It is the river of life flowing again into the cold, hardened valleys of a once-embittered heart. Forgiveness is at the core and is the essence of revival itself.

Whenever pardon is abundantly given, there is a definite and occasionally dramatic release of life against the powers of death in the heavenly places. Observe the release of life when Jesus, on the cross, prayed, **"Father, forgive them"** (Luke 23:34). At that very moment every demonic principality and power which had infiltrated man's relationship with God was **"disarmed!"** (Col 2:15) As the spikes were driven into the palms and feet of the Savior, and as He pleaded, **"they do not know what they are doing"** (Luke 23:34), hell's gates unlocked, tombs opened, the veil into the holy place rent, and heaven itself opened—all because of His forgiveness. Even many dead arose (see Matthew 27:51-53). The hand of God shattered boundaries in every known dimension through the power released when Christ forgave our sins.

Jesus, on the cross, **"canceled out [our] certificate of debt"** (Col 2:14). By His act of forgiveness, He simultaneously disarmed **"the rulers and authorities"** (v 15). Likewise, when *we* forgive there is a canceling of debts and a disarming of the enemy. You see, Christ's forgiveness disarmed the devil in mankind's heavenward relationship with God; our pardon of others disarms the enemy in our earthly relationships toward one another!

Consider the last time you experienced full healing in a severed relationship. It is likely that such words as "wonderful" and "glorious" were used to describe the baptism of love that renewed your souls. Can we see that forgiveness is the very heart of Christ's message?

Several years ago I met an Islamic scientist from India. Islam is a religion based on man's righteousness, and he had stumbled over the lack of "good works" among the Christians he knew. As I witnessed to him, I soon found myself in a debate concerning the credibility of Christianity. As our discussion grew mutually more ardent, two of my children approached; one was crying, the other angry.

My procedure in disciplining the children is to have a brief "hearing" in which I judge both sides of the conflict. I discern who is the victim and who is the offender, and I have the victim pass sentence on the offender. I ask, "How many spankings should I give?" The victim knows that next week the roles may be reversed and he or she may be the culprit in need of pardon. Thus the wounded child extends mercy and says, "No spankings." The result is that the kindness of the victim leads the offender to repentance. As the judge, I did not have to punish the guilty because the debt was canceled; the victim's mercy triumphed over judgment. The result is that enmity is broken, children are reconciled, and friendship is restored.

Our "trial" was over quickly, and the children were happy once again. All this had taken place while my Muslim friend watched, and when I turned back to him to continue our debate, he said, "There is no need to continue. I have just seen the power of Christianity!"

One of the most fundamental truths of our faith is that through Christ we have received forgiveness from God for sins, and because of Christ we can forgive one another. Someone pays the price to absorb the offense to themselves, but in so doing they release the power of God, bringing healing to souls. It may rend the heavens, as Christ's forgiveness did for us, or it may rend the heart when we forgive one another. Whether the result is spectacular or subtle, however, forgiveness is the very life of God!

When Stephen forgave his murderers, a plea for mercy with "Saul of Tarsus" written on it ascended to the heart of God. Could it have been the divine response to Stephen's forgiveness that was instrumental in transforming Saul into Paul, an apostle of God?

Consider the reunion of Jacob and Esau. Esau is known in the Scriptures as a hardened man, one who sold his birthright for a single meal. Yet as Jacob bowed seven times to the ground in repentance, asking forgiveness from Esau, a flow of life from the heart of God flooded the embittered Esau. Scripture tells us there was such a release of grace into his soul that he **"ran to meet [Jacob] and embraced him, and fell on his neck and kissed him, and they wept"** (Gen 33:4). Esau's heart melted, and he chose to forgive the repentant Jacob. So moved was he that he ran and embraced Jacob, kissed him, and then wept on his neck. When we truly desire to walk in repentance and reconciliation, *even a man as hardened as Esau can be touched by God!*

We see this divine flow of life again when Joseph was reunited with his brothers. Having been sold by them into slavery, Joseph had every right to be bitter. Instead he chose to forgive. Note carefully the washing of the Spirit of God through these lives as Joseph was reconciled with his brothers:

> **Then Joseph could not control himself . . . And he wept so loudly that the Egyptians heard it, and the household of Pharaoh heard of it. Then Joseph said to his brothers, "I am Joseph!"** (Gen 45:1-3)

Joseph was so full of love and for-giveness that he actually begged his guilt-laden brothers to forgive themselves. He pleaded, **"Do not be grieved or angry with yourselves . . . for God sent me before you to preserve life . . . and to keep you alive by a great deliverance"** (vv 5, 7).

There was no bitterness, no revenge, no angry last word which preceded his forgiveness. There was only the foretaste of Christ's own unconditional forgiveness to every self-condemned sinner. Indeed, like Joseph, every time we forgive we too **"preserve life."** We restore our brethren to wholeness **"by a great deliverance."**

Release Every Man His Servant

Forgiveness is the very spirit of heaven removing the hiding places of demonic activity from the caverns of the human soul. It is every wrong made right and every evil redeemed for good. The power released in forgiveness is actually a mighty weapon in the war to save our cities.

Jeremiah 34 unveils the impact of wholesale forgiveness upon a city, reveal-ing what might have happened had the Jews obeyed God's call of release. The account speaks of more than the recon-ciliation of family relationships. It deals with the entire city of Jerusalem as well as all the cities of Judah. It reveals the wonderful wisdom and love of God in His willingness to save His stubborn, sinful people.

The story occurs at a time when the Israelites were hopelessly outnumbered. Seemingly every enemy who could carry a sword had it pointed at their cities. We read that

Nebuchadnezzar king of Babylon and all his army, with all the kingdoms of the earth that were under his dominion and all the peoples, were fighting against Jerusalem and against all its cities (Jer 34:1).

Is this not our battle as well? Do we not have our own "king of Babylon" with his hosts set against us (see Revelation 17-18)? We see armies of demons led by principalities attacking and almost over-running city after city. The demonic powers of immorality, rebellion, drugs, rock music, satanism, greed, murder, and fear have all but swallowed up many of our larger communities. Unless the Lord acts mightily, will we not continue to be overwhelmed by the dimensions of the battle?

Such was the plight of Israel. Yet hidden in the ways of God was a plan, a strategy, which would both rout the enemy and heal their cities. The Lord called them to implement the "year of remission," which proclaimed complete and generous release to both servants and slaves (see Deuteronomy 15:1-18).

Then Jeremiah the prophet spoke all these words to Zedekiah king of Judah . . . that each man should set free his male servant and each man his female servant, a Hebrew man or a Hebrew woman; so that no one should keep them, a Jew his brother, in bondage. And all the officials and all the people obeyed, who had entered into the covenant that each man should set free his male servant and each man his female servant, so that no one should keep them any longer in bondage; they obeyed, and set them free (Jer 34:6-10).

It is one thing to have lost at war and thus become the slave of an enemy, but it is quite another to become the slave of your brother. Yet this kind of servitude was a provision of the Mosaic Law. One's indebtedness could enslave him to another.

However, every seven years Jews who were slaves were to be released, and every fiftieth year all their original properties were to be returned. However, in all the years since the law of remission was issued, Israel has never celebrated this Jubilee, and only rarely has an individual released his slaves. Yet at the time Jeremiah spoke this to the king, even with their enemies within striking range, the

Notes

entire nation set about to free every man his slave.

How does this story relate to us? Whenever any relationship exists outside the shelter of covering love, it degenerates into a system of mutual expectations and unwritten laws to which we all become debtors. As it was under the Law of Moses, so also it is in the context of human relationships: indebtedness enslaves. Obviously, we do not enact the master/slave relationship, but our unforgiving opinion of the offender enslaves him, together with his offense, in our memory.

It is a basic principle of life: Where there is no love, of necessity there must be law. And where there is law, there are both debts and debtors. To counter the debilitating effect indebtedness has upon relationships, Jesus commanded His disciples to maintain love among all men. For love transcends the "ledger sheet mentality"; it refuses to **"take into account a wrong suffered"** (1 Cor 13:5).

How shall we deal with debts? Christ warned we would not be forgiven unless we forgave others. Whenever we are unforgiving, we are also reacting. Those unChristlike reactions to offenses become our sin before God. To be released from our reactions we must return to the cause, the first offense, and be reconciled. As we forgive, we are forgiven and restored; life and balance return to our souls.

In our story from Jeremiah, the Judeans did not merely forgive each other; they made a **"covenant"** before God. They cut a calf in two, and they passed **"between its parts"** (Jer 34:18). This was the same kind of quality covenant relationship Abraham had made centuries earlier with the Lord (see Genesis 15:10,17,18). They made a covenant with God to release one another!

The redemptive plan of God was this: If the Israelites set free their slaves, they would not be taken as slaves. If they showed mercy, He would show Himself merciful as well. The destruction of their cities would be averted, for **"mercy triumphs over judgment"** (James 2:13). Although they were sinners, love would fulfill the law and make all things clean for them (see Galatians 5:14; Luke 11:41).

Look what happened to the Judeans' enemies as the populace enacted the covenant of remission. Something marvelous was occurring in the spirit realm. Supernaturally the Lord drew **"the king of Babylon . . . away"** (Jer 34:21). At the very moment the people were being merciful to one another and releasing their slaves, their enemy was drawn away and their war ended! What they did on earth was actually being done for them in the heavens.

We are just like the Judeans of Jeremiah's day. Our cities are also under attack, and no program or government aid

Notes

can help us. What we need desperately is divine intervention and deliverance. We need to see the mercy of God and His convicting power poured out supernaturally on the people!

Some may say our cities are like Sodom—beyond saving, beyond redemption. This argument usually arises from a heart whose love has grown weak. Yet the first cause of sin in Sodom was a lack of mercy. He said,

> **"Behold, this was the guilt of your sister Sodom: she and her daughters had arrogance, abundant food, and careless ease, but she did not help the poor and needy. Thus they were haughty and committed abominations before Me. Therefore I removed them when I saw it"** (Ezek 16:49-50).

This prophecy concerning Sodom came from Ezekiel, who was Jeremiah's contemporary. He was probably speaking to many of these same people who later released their slaves! The root sin, the cause of Sodom's wickedness, was not perversity but selfishness. It was a city full of wealth but without mercy, refusing to help the poor and needy. Thus, they went on to commit abominations before the Lord. Any society that hardens its heart toward mercy opens its heart toward hell. But when a people become merciful, mercy is allotted to them.

The appeal of God is that we return to love and forgiveness. The Israelites, like the Sodomites, had fallen far short of the Lord's standard of righteousness, as we have done also. Yet, for all their sins, God had one more plan, one more divine alternative, that might have completely changed the end of the book of Jeremiah and brought lasting deliverance. It was pure, and it was simple. The Lord called for a covenant of forgiveness; His plan was to flood the heavenlies with mercy. The very mercy the Judeans were giving to each other would pave the way for God to show mercy toward them, and it worked: The King of Babylon, his armies, and every one of Israel's enemies left the nation!

They Fell from Grace

The Lord gave the Judeans one last opportunity, but when their enemies left and the pressure upon them abated, they did something terrible. Instead of maintaining their mercy, they brought their brothers back into slavery.

> **But afterward they turned around and took back the male servants and the female servants, whom they had set free, and brought them into subjection for male servants and for female servants** (Jer 34:11).

Under the fear of death they released their slaves. Now, with the threat of

Notes

death removed, they returned to their self-ishness.

We need to understand that where there is a decrease of love there will be an increase of demonic activity in our relationships. The Jews released their slaves, and the enemy left. But like so many of us, when the pressure was removed, they returned to their sin: They took back their slaves!

> **"Therefore thus says the Lord, 'You have not obeyed Me in proclaiming release each man to his brother, and each man to his neighbor. Behold . . . I will give [you] into the hand of those who seek [your] life, and into the hand of the army of the king of Babylon which has gone away from you. Behold, I am going to command,' declares the Lord, 'and I will bring them back to this city; and they shall fight against it and take it' "** (Jer 34:17,21-22).

The Lord gave them exactly what they gave each other. They made their brethren slaves; their enemies in turn made them slaves. It is ironic that when Israel was finally carried off into Babylon, a number of these very slaves were left in the land. Many of the individuals who had been re-enslaved were assigned the properties of their former masters.

But do not be mistaken. As the book of Lamentations testifies, this was no happy ending. However, for us the final outcome of the war against our cities is yet to be written. There is still time to flood the heavens with the mercies of God. If there is citywide repentance for unforgiveness, even "Esaus" will fall weeping upon the necks of their brothers. If there is a canceling of debts, deliverance can come as it did to Joseph's brothers, even to those who are guilty of betrayal. Wherever love prevails, the strongholds of hell will be torn down, and the spiritual armies surrounding our cities will be disarmed.

This release of divine power is resident even now in our capacity to set one another free from indebtedness. All we must do is forgive our debtors and maintain the attitude of forgiveness. As we release each other, God Himself will begin to release our brethren, our churches, and ultimately our cities. It is up to us, as individuals, to flood the spirit realms with mercy. For whatever we loose on earth will be loosed and given back to us in the heavenlies.

Let's pray: *Father, we have sinned against You and against our brethren. By our lack of mercy, through the hardness of our hearts toward our brethren, we have allowed the devil access to the church and to our cities; we have brought judgment to our land. Forgive us, Lord! In all sincerity, we make a covenant of forgiveness with You*

Notes

Notes

and all men. We choose, as did Jesus, to absorb the debt unto ourselves and free one another. As we release one another, liberate us from the grip of our enemy. As we show mercy, pour Your mercy upon our cities! In Jesus' name. Amen.

Discipleship Training Booklets

truths compiled from the writings of Francis Frangipane
$2.50 each
10 or more–40% discount, 50 or more–50% discount